# Grabbing the Heel of Destiny

*By: Dennis Paul Goldsworthy-Davis*

Open Wells Ministries

15315 Capital Port

Sam Antonio, TX  78249

www.openwellsministries.org

# PREFACE

Just as this book is centered on a man that wouldn't let go of his destiny so it has been my journey which, by God's good grace, is still my journey. It was God's destiny within me that drove me into the ministry and equally sent me across the seas from England to live in the States. My wife used to say to me, "You are so Irish, you just won't give in!"

My reply was and is, "It's not the Irish in me. It's the Holy Spirit who won't let me go." The scriptures say,

> *"...being confident of this, that He who began a good work in you will carry it on until the day of Christ Jesus."* Philippians 1:6

Grabbing the heel of destiny sounds like the act of a person that knew what his existence was for. Actually, he changed the destiny of Israel. So can we affect not only ourselves but those around us and those who follow us. So many give in so easily but we need to not let go. That has been my life and motto. I want to finish my course as Paul finished his! David pursued and Paul pursued and so did Elisha. The list goes on! Will we?

I know, as the book states, that God has put it within you, but will you follow it? Will you chase it? Will you make it yours?

# OTHER BOOKS BY
## DENNIS PAUL GOLDSWORTHY-DAVIS

## Available on Amazon.com

*Grace Looks Good on You*

*Touching the God of Jacob*

*Standing in the Perfect Storm*

*Gaining the Commanded Blessings*

*Unlimited Anointing: Secrets to Operating in the Fullness of God's Power*

*Walking in the Prophetic*

©2022 by Open Wells Ministries

No part of this book, written or graphic, may be reproduced by any means whatsoever, mechanical or electronic, without written permission from the publisher,
Open Wells Ministries, 15315 Capital Port, San Antonio, TX 78249

Library of Congress Number:

ISBN: 978-1-7355716-5-2

Printed in the United States of America by Open Wells Ministries

Scripture references were taken from:

THE HOLY BIBLE, NEW INTERNATIONAL VERSION®, NIV® Copyright © 1973, 1978, 1984, 2011 by Biblica, Inc.® Used by permission. All rights reserved worldwide.

KING JAMES VERSION

REFERENCES ARE PUBLIC DOMAIN IN THE US

# Contents

*By: Dennis Paul Goldsworthy-Davis*

PREFACE

OTHER BOOKS BY

DENNIS PAUL GOLDSWORTHY-DAVIS

TABLE OF CONTENTS

FOREWORD

BY Dr. Greg Hood

INTRODUCTION

CHAPTER 1

Destined From Birth

CHAPTER 2

A Greater Purpose

That Reveals Greater Purpose

CHAPTER 3

The Hand That Grabbed the Foot

CHAPTER 4

My Heart is Stirred by a Noble Theme

CHAPTER 5

Learning to Pursue

CHAPTER 6

I Clung to Him

and Would Not Let Him Go

CHAPTER 7

From the Days of John the Baptist Until Now

CHAPTER 8

What is That You See
CHAPTER 9
We Must Not Let Go
CHAPTER 10
That Moment of Faith
CHAPTER 11
Walking in Destiny's Fulfillment
TESTIMONIES
BIOGRAPHY

# FOREWORD
## BY Dr. Greg Hood

Who am I? Why am I here? What is my purpose? These questions are among the oldest put forth by honest men and women who are seeking answers to the age-old question, "What is life about?"

It is a hapless truth that many people live with a quiet hopelessness and some die tortured by the blurred uneasiness that somehow they have "missed it". Others wander aimlessly—a few purposefully—attempting to find the right answers to these million-dollar questions.

Many Believers have declared that salvation is the "be all and end all" of life here. Being born-again is not the "be all and end all" of life. It is the entrance to the Kingdom of God. There are many "truly saved" Believers who feel unfulfilled, even as they wrestle with oneself, fasting and praying in an attempt to quiet the nagging sense that there must be something more to life. Yes, they know Yeshua. Yes, many have been filled with Holy Spirit. Still, the great majority wonder, "What lies beyond salvation and the baptism of Holy Spirit?".

Unfortunately, many born-again believers never make it out

of this world with these questions answered. They never get to walk out their God-given purpose. They take all of that embodied wealth with them when they leave this world. They were never taught to pursue their destiny. They were never told that they could become the very thing they dreamed of being. You see, I believe the wealthiest place on the planet is the graveyard. There are so many inventions, books, sermons, business ideas, political seats of offices left vacant, songs, awards, mentorships and investments deposited into the grave with those who never had hope or who were full of fear and never walked out their destiny. Don't let this happen to you. Grab the heel of your destiny and live your purpose!

You must know that God has a purpose for your life. Jeremiah 29:11 tells us this quite directly:

*"For I know the plans that I have for you, declares the Lord, plans for welfare and not calamity to give you a future and a hope." (NASB)*

This passage will empower you to release faith into your heart in the most powerful way. God has a plan for me? God has prepared things for me? God has been dreaming about me and my future? YES! He didn't bring you into this earth to just pass time. His intentions are not for you to become stagnant in some hopeless, mundane cycle of life that produces no fruit of your destiny. No, He birthed you for PURPOSE!

My friend, Dennis Goldsworthy-Davis, in *Grabbing the Heel of Destiny*, goes a long way toward answering these very important life questions. No single book except the Bible can answer all your questions, but drawing from the wellspring of divine revelation, life experience, and prophetic insight, Dennis has cut a path with this book that will launch you in the direction of fulfillment, while providing the answer to the all-encompassing question, "Why am I here?"

You have not picked up this book by accident. You haven't wandered here without "purpose". There is modus operandi to this journey and clues are at hand. Perhaps, you will find in these pages what you have been seeking for years—purpose. So, I decree that as you dive into these pages filled with prophetic revelation, you will begin to discover your prophetic blue print. I decree that you will begin to live from the power of your true identity. I decree over you, when you leave this earth you will leave empty! Nothing will be deposited in the graveyard. All of the wealth that you embody will be spent up during your lifetime. I decree this book will empower you to discover your purpose and live out your true destiny.

Now, get your pen and paper; ready yourself you take notes as you journey through this great work, *Grabbing the Heel of Destiny*.

Dr. Greg Hood, Th.D.
Author, The *Gospel of the Kingdom* and *Rebuilding the Broken Altar: Awakening out of Chaos*
Apostolic Overseer - The Network of Five-fold Ministers and Churches
Founder and President of Kingdom University and Greg Hood Ministries
www.GregHood.org
www.KingdomU.org

# INTRODUCTION

*Grabbing the Heel of Destiny*, what a title! Where did that come from? It came from the Lord speaking to me one morning and quoting this very statement. I knew he was directing me to how Jacob grabbed his brother's heel coming from the womb in Genesis 25, but clearly he wanted us to learn not only what our purpose is but to learn how to grasp it. To do so, firstly we must deal with what often is an identity crisis. Many are feeling lost in the mass of humanity around us. For those of us alive in this 21st Century, we live in a day and age where the population is growing exponentially. With over 7 billion people on the earth today and the growth not slowing down, one might feel like an ant in an ant hill, like sand on the sea shore and a star in the sky. One only has to walk through the streets of New York or London to feel like one of the minions passing through. So, quoting from one of my friends, "We can truly feel lost in the vastness of it all." But should we feel so lost or is there a destiny for each one of us? Was there a real purpose for my being born? Did the God who spoke to Jeremiah also know me before I was formed?

*"Before I formed you in the womb..."* Jeremiah 1:5

If it is true for one, surely it is true for all? Surely he is the same God? But is destiny just for special people, the selected ones, the ones destined to be famous or is God who he says he is?

> *"Then Peter began to speak: 'I now realize how true it is that God does not show favoritism but accepts from every nation the one who fears him and does what is right.'"* Acts 10:34-35

The Lord has spoken such a wonderful revelation in the book of Acts to answer all this! Paul, challenging the Greeks on their view of life makes this incredible statement,

> *"From one man he made all the nations, that they should inhabit the whole earth; and he marked out their appointed times in history and the boundaries of their lands."* Acts 17:26

Another version says,

> *"He decided exactly when and where they should live."* Acts 17:26 ERV

THERE IT IS! Your life is predestined and pre-purposed!

Now that is clearly established let's look at the rest of what the Lord said to Jeremiah.

> *"…I knew you, before you were born I set you apart; I appointed you as a prophet to the nations."* Jeremiah 1:5

That sounds like destiny to me. The purpose might be different, the appointing different but the God who formed us did it for purpose.

We all might wish that we lived in a different time in history but that is not what the Lord had planned. Equally important is that he knows best where to place us for his purpose and where we can bear the fruit in life that he intended.

Once this becomes clear, we must learn to grasp the heel of destiny that is offered to us.

# CHAPTER 1

# Destined From Birth

The Bible so often speaks of people before they were born. The paramount one, of course, is Jesus. He is spoken of all over the Bible. Then we see the prophet announce John the Baptist including an angel visitation in Luke Chapter 1. He was clearly born for purpose. We have already referenced how Jeremiah was purposed of God. Then there is Sampson in Judges 13. Of course, there is the story of Jacob.

> *"The babies jostled each other within her...So she went to inquire of the Lord. The Lord said to her, 'Two nations are in your womb, and two peoples from within you will be separated; one people will be stronger than the other, and the older will serve the younger.'"* Genesis 25:22-23.

Jacob wrestled with his brother in the womb.

> *"The first to come out was red, and his whole body was like a hairy garment; so they named him Esau. After this, his brother came out, with his hand grasping Esau's heel; so he was named Jacob."* Genesis 25:25-26

That wrestle continued in birth and throughout life until Jacob realized his full destiny.

What these examples and others like them do is point out the purposes of God in the lives of men and women in a predestined manner. No, I declare, we were not just the plan or accident of parents but a plan by the creator of all things of higher purpose and destiny.

While being used prophetically in my life, I have had many situations where I would hear a baby crying while standing next to a young woman who was not yet pregnant. Often very soon afterward we heard that she was pregnant. I have then seen these same women become mothers not long after. Where did this gift come from? I worked as a young pastor in Bristol, England, and was privileged to be part of a team where one of the ladies was born after Smith Wigglesworth prayed for her seemingly barren mother. The faith and anointing for this ministry were passed on to me. Having seen this many times, it is clear that the Lord is involved in our births and destinies more deeply than we have given thought to. That is why abortion is so incredibly sad, stopping the potential of a life of purpose and destiny.

In order for God to point us to destiny and purpose, he many times has to bring such healing in our lives. A child, feeling something deep in their heart and knowing something of eternal value is beginning to form in them, can be abused verbally or in other ways causing them to redirect their lives in order to deal with the pain and rejection. Jesus came to,

> *"...bind up the brokenhearted, to proclaim freedom for the captives and release from darkness for the prisoners."* Isaiah 61:1

My own father who was 12 years military, sadly affected me as a young man. He did many good things like taking me to church Though I did feel something deep in my heart of purpose, he verbally said things and did things that affected me. All I wanted to do was to pay everyone back. I became one that you would not have wanted to meet until I met Christ and his healing.

Worry not! The God of destiny will work things out for his purpose. He knows how to find us, follow us and chase us down. He knows what rabbit holes we have gone down, what walls we have built up. If he got me and got David and the apostle Paul, he can get you too!

I thought a great modern-day example could be given to encourage in this. Tim Tebow, known to so many as a college success and then later in the professional football scene, was born because his mother knew he had a destiny even though she was told to abort due to complications. She stood her ground, the miracle happened and now he is affecting so many. Destiny in the womb overcame natural circumstances. First a mother and now this young man grasped the heel of destiny!

The story of Moses, recorded in Exodus Chapter 2, is quite fascinating. He was born during the time that Egypt was killing the Hebrew children. When Moses was born his mother saw that he was a fine child.

> *"When she saw that he was a fine child, she hid him for three months."* Exodus 2:2

The King James Version translates that he was a *"Goodly child"*. Clearly there was a sense of destiny all over him. According to the story in Exodus 2:3-10, His mother grabs the heal of destiny and hides him for three months. When she can't hide him any longer she makes a little ark of bulrushes and places him on the Nile, trusting God to keep him safe. Along comes Pharaoh's daughter and discovers him. Eventually she unknowingly hands him back to his own mother to nurse and then raises him as a prince in the palace. Destiny? Purpose? There it is! Raised as a prince so that he could lead a people! If we were to go back through our lives what would we see of the hand of God keeping us, saving us and steering us toward our God given destiny!

# CHAPTER 2

# A Greater Purpose That Reveals Greater Purpose

We have the destiny to become the sons of God! When we have the joy of meeting The Lord Jesus Christ, it opens up a greater destiny than ever before. Actually, according to the scriptures and before even time as we know it began, God had planned this for us. Ephesians is a fantastic revelation of this.

> *"For he chose us in him before the creation of the world to be holy and blameless in his sight. In love he predestined us for adoption to sonship through Jesus Christ, in accordance with his pleasure and will."* Ephesians 1:4-5

In other words, God preplanned our salvation and sonship. The next few verses speak of his lavishing his grace on us to accomplish this. We had a destiny planned with our names on it. God predestined that through the sacrifice of Jesus we could become his sons, too! Hebrews tells us this explicitly.

> *"In bringing many sons and daughters to glory, it was fitting that God, for whom and through whom everything exists, should make the pioneer of their salvation perfect through what he suffered."*
> Hebrews 2:10

Now this opens up a greater purpose than we could have imagined. With sonship comes inheritance. But how do we find this inheritance? Well, according to the book of Romans, the Holy Spirit leads us into this inheritance.

> *"For those who are led by the Spirit of God are the children of God.... the Spirit you received brought about your adoption to sonship...The Spirit himself testifies with our spirit that we are God's children. Now if we are children, then we are heirs—heirs of God and co-heirs with Christ..."* Romans 8:14-17

It is the Holy Spirit that reveals purpose and destiny and inheritance to us. In 1 Corinthians 2, we read an amazing revelation. The Holy Spirit searches the deep things of God planned for us and reveals them to us! That is destiny awakened!

> *"What no eye has seen, what no ear has heard, and what no human mind has conceived the things God*

> *has prepared for those who love him—these are the things God has revealed to us by his Spirit. The Spirit searches all things, even the deep things of God."* 1 Corinthians 2:9-10

Dreams and visions are given us by the same Holy Spirit!

> *"'And afterward, I will pour out my Spirit on all people. Your sons and daughters will prophesy, your old men will dream dreams, your young men will see visions.'"* Joel 2:28

The word for *dreams and visions* here is a word that means *to become heavy with or to carry*. Yes, he makes you pregnant with purpose.

He works through your imagination and desires.

> *"Now to him who is able to do immeasurably more than all we ask or imagine, according to his power that is at work within us..."* Ephesians 3:20

Clearly the Holy Spirit awakens us to our God given destiny and purpose. The Holy Spirit reveals and stirs the direction of our fulfilling this statement Jesus himself made:

> *"You did not choose me, but I chose you and appointed you so that you might go and bear fruit- fruit that will last."* John 15:16

To grasp the heel of destiny we must search out our destiny and calling and respond to it with The Spirit's help. We must respond both to what we are shown and what we are given. One of my favorite cries found in the Bible is so relevant:

> *"Where now is the Lord, the God of Elijah?"*
> 2 Kings 2:14

This is Elisha picking up the cloak of his forerunner, Elijah! He puts it to the test. His attitude is that if Elijah says it's his and says he is to own this cloak with its anointing, well then, he will put it to the test. LET'S DO THIS! LET'S GO FOR IT! Let's try it on for size, this destiny I have been promised to walk in.

# CHAPTER 3

# The Hand That Grabbed the Foot

What a sight it must have been: a baby born red and hairy all over! In fact, the Bible says that hair looked like a garment. Then suddenly you see a hand reaching out and grabbing this hairy red baby by the heel.

> *"The first to come out was red, and his whole body was like a hairy garment; so they named him Esau."* Genesis 25:25

That, my friends, would have made headlines anywhere in the world. Rather, it has been recorded in God's word for billions to see it through thousands of years. What on earth is going on? Earlier in the Chapter it says the babies jostled in the womb, like a wrestling match. The mother, being so disturbed, asked the Lord what was happening. He answered,

> *"Two nations are in your womb, and two peoples from within you will be separated; one people will be stronger than the other, and the older will serve the younger!"* Genesis 25:23

The younger brother was trying to displace the older one so that he could take his rightful place. WHEN HE GRABBED HIS HEEL, HE WAS REACHING OUT FOR HIS GOD GIVEN DESTINY!

There is nothing like the grip of a baby! It is called *baby grasp reflex*. People love it but it is a God given reflex that is later exchanged for more normal grasping. This baby, Jacob, was using a God given reflex to grab onto what was his destiny! This needs to become our reflex, too. Once we begin to feel our purpose and destiny we should, like a baby, reach out to God. We should grab onto our promise and not let go. So often, when we receive a promise or a dream, we have a tendency to place it on a shelf. But watch Elisha! He ran after the mantle that touched him in 1 Kings 19. Watch how David said,

> *"My soul followeth hard after thee…"* Psalm 63:8 KJV

Then consider this statement from Paul

> *"…but I press on to take hold of that for which Christ Jesus took hold of me."* Philippians 3: 12-14

The word *press* there is *like that of a hunter chasing its foe*. We are involved in our own destiny and must become hungry for it to be fulfilled. One of the funniest things that ever happened to me when I first came to the States was when I went fishing with a man who was much bigger and heavier than I was. His line became tangled so we had to take the boat we were in back to the dock. His weight made the boat pull away from the dock. I leant out to grab it and was stretched to my fullest just hanging on by my fingers. It must have looked hilarious. At least my friend thought so! He was laughing so loud as just by my pure finger strength I held the boat and then began with my fingers to pull it back in. There is that grip I found as a baby. Now it helped me get the boat back. How much more this help when we learn to grab and not let go in regard to our destiny.

The Greek word most used for *to receive* is a word called *Lambano*. Its base meaning is *to take what is offered*. When you add *Kata* to it and make the word *Katalambano* it means *to take hold of or make it your own* or *to GRASP or GRAB*. This word is used by Paul quite a few times but the passage in Philippians that we have already looked at uses it twice and is totally relevant for this book. My summary of Philippians 3:12 is this: God took hold of me, now I must take hold of what he took hold of me for. I MUST GRAB THE HEEL OF DESTINY.

Has God taken hold of you? Has destiny touched you? Have you received a promise? Then you must grasp it and not let it go, until it becomes yours.

# CHAPTER 4

# My Heart is Stirred by a Noble Theme

One of my favorite songs of yesteryear, was the song whose first verse was birthed from this Psalm:

> *"My heart is stirred by a noble theme."* Psalm 45:1

Nobility, meaning nothing less than the King himself stirring the heart toward a noble purpose and destiny. A kingly stirring. There is nothing more noble than that.

Stirring by God is used all over the Bible. He even stirred kings and leaders toward purpose. But the psalmist tells us clearly where he is stirred.

> *"...He has also set eternity in the human heart..."*
> Ecclesiastes 3:11

God stirs up the heart. His methods are many. He stirs by dreams, prophesies or by just plain moving the heart but whichever is the method, the aim is the same. The heart is stirred by nobility and for noble purposes. This verse was written by the sons of Korah. It is clearly written by one of David's spiritual sons who was part of the greatest worship team ever to have stood on the face of the earth. But what about God stirring a heart yet in the womb? What about placing destiny in an unborn babe to the degree that he reached out his hand to grab the heel of his brother, signifying that this would be his lifestyle until he gained what he had been stirred to own in God?

What is so amazing about these stirrings is that even unsaved men and women through the ages have been affected by them. God always works in the heart of man, yet how much more toward a Godly destiny? For instance: God has set eternity in the heart of man, which means all men are stirred toward eternal things but then there is the stirring toward personal purpose. Jesus manifested it at 12 years of age:

> *"'Why are you searching for me?' he asked. 'Didn't you know I had to be in my Father's house?'"* Luke 2:49

John the Baptist manifested it in the womb:

> *"As soon as the sound of your greeting reached my ears the baby in my womb leaped for joy."* Luke 1:44.

David's purpose was shown when he was nothing more than a young lad in the field:

> *"...the Lord has sought out a man after his own heart and appointed him ruler of his people..."* Samuel 13:14

And then there is the story of Samuel in 1 Samuel chapter 3. He learned to minister before God before he even knew his voice. History tells us of both the Wesleys and George Whitfield being in prayer meetings before they truly met God. The list of those whose purpose was set in their hearts goes on and on.

I personally knew these stirrings both toward the Lord and his purpose at a young age. I felt stirred toward standing on platforms and stirred toward flying before I knew the Lord. After I got saved when he wanted me to preach and travel the stirring got more intense. WOW! This was before he confirmed my purpose with his word and visions. My heart had been stirred by a noble theme. Has yours? If so, you cannot become dormant. You must grasp the heel of destiny. I personally experienced hearing this word when being sent from England to America:

> *"Who has stirred up one from the east, calling him in righteousness to his service."* Isaiah 41:2

He even put America in my heart to bring me from one nation to another for his purpose.

Let your heart be stirred by such a noble theme. Ask the Lord to even resurrect that which might have become dormant or silent within you.

# CHAPTER 5

# Learning to Pursue

From the moment the heart of the child, Jacob, picked up his purpose he instantly began to pursue that purpose. This is seen throughout scripture. David also cries out,

> *"My soul followeth hard after thee..."*
> Psalm 63:8 KJV

This was relative to circumstance and desire. His attitude is clearly that of grabbing the heel of his destiny. In fact, one of the greatest testimonies is that given by God himself to David when Samuel spoke of him being a man after God's own heart in 1 Samuel 13:14. A heart like God's, chasing God and affected by God. He is clearly recorded as a real live God-chaser. David did this throughout his whole life. He sought God before he was anointed to be king. Why? Because he knew before he was anointed. He knew before he was singled out. The destiny had been set in his heart! Did he know the details? Only eternity will reveal that but he knew something, that is for sure. He never stopped chasing the fullness of his destiny and that should be our desire! Don't stop halfway! Grab hold!

Many others are worthy of mention but perhaps the statement of Paul to the Philippians must now be followed. Here is a man who was already an apostle, had already seen Jesus, had already worked mighty miracles and had been taken into heaven and yet still makes this remarkable statement:

> *"Not that I have already obtained all this, or have already arrived at my goal, but I press on to take hold of that for which Christ Jesus took hold of me."* Philippians 3:12

The word *press* here is likened to *a hunter chasing a foe or deer*. The statement, "to take hold"? Wow! That means I want to grab it, grasp it and obtain it! There it is, my friends. Paul who had already obtained and done so much knew that God wanted more for him. Why? Because the Lord had taken hold of him for more. What has the Lord taken hold of us for? Are we willing to pursue and chase until we grab hold of all that is ours? Paul shows us how important this had become to him. He would let no previous success or failure get in the way, like a runner pushing for the tape in his quest to grasp all that he was destined to be!

> *"Brothers and sisters, I do not consider myself yet to have taken hold of it. But one thing I do: Forgetting what is behind and straining toward what is ahead, I press on toward the goal to win the prize for which God has called me heavenward in Christ Jesus."* Philippians 3:13-14

This is the way we grab our heel of destiny! Whether a calling, a relationship or all that has been promised to us WE ARE INVOLVED! We must pursue and pursue until we have that which is ours. Doris Day used to sing that famous song titled *Whatever Will Be, Will Be (Qué Será, Será)*. No! Not true! We must chase what is promised until we have it and not sit around waiting on chance.

May God grant us a heart that responds to all that has been put in it and will not let go until it obtains it to the fullest degree.

# CHAPTER 6

# I Clung to Him and Would Not Let Him Go

This statement actually comes from the Song of Solomon. What a book of relationship and growth! In the first 5 verses of chapter 3, the bride had become complacent in her relationship with the groom as so often the church does. She was waiting for him to come to her on her bed but this time he didn't come. She realized if this relationship was to go on she must get up and search for him. She eventually found him and when she did she clung to him and would not let him go. What a fantastic analogy of the church! But it is this statement that is so relevant to this book:

> *"...when I found the one my heart loves. I held him and would not let him go..."* Song of Solomon 3:4

Once reunited she wasn't going to let it go again. No! Not again! This speaks, too, of grabbing the heel of destiny. Listen to her statement, the intent and the longing to fulfill her God given destiny with him.

Many years ago I went on a mission to Malaysia and Singapore. I went through quite a torrid time getting home. The plane was brought down with a hydraulic failure. Quite an experience to say the least. I was shuffled to a hotel in Malaysia and then flown to Karachi in Pakistan. This was before cell phones. I thought the airline had notified my wife. I didn't have money for a call back to England and couldn't figure out in those days how to do a reverse charge call. The airline was not being helpful at all. She didn't know where I was! I disappeared for about three days. She went to the airport in London every day for three days which was quite a journey, indeed. No Dennis! The airline didn't know where I was. She was petrified and called for prayer all over England. On the fourth day I arrived and she was there at the airport again. When she saw me she shrieked out and ran through the crowd and clung to me. She wouldn't let me go. Her grip was so strong! It was the grip of desperation.

My story, though a little different to the Song of Solomon, is such a great illustration. In the Song the bride searched and searched. In life my wife searched and searched. The answer? Both brides found their man and wouldn't let go. We must have that attitude when it comes to our destiny and purpose! Search for it and cling to it.

Now back to our friend Jacob and the infamous wrestle with the Angel of the Lord in Genesis 32:24-31. He makes this incredible statement,

> *"I will not let you go unless you bless me."*
> Genesis 32:26

Wow, where did that come from? He had waited since birth to grasp his destiny and now he was being asked to let go, to back off! Are you for real? This is the one whose hand grabbed his brother's heel! He was not letting anyone go! NOT UNTIL YOU BLESS ME! There it is! Not until what I know is mine becomes mine! Costly? Read the story. He came out limping but he came out blessed!

"Then the man said, 'Your name will no longer be Jacob, but Israel'...Then he blessed him there." Genesis 32:28-29

He came out with a new name that was a history changing name but all because he would not let go!

WE MUST NOT LET GO. God put it in you so that you would wrestle for it, claim it, pray it and refuse to let it go.

# CHAPTER 7

# From the Days of John the Baptist Until Now

Anyone who has read the gospels will have run into the fascinating scripture spoken, of course, by Jesus!

> *"And from the days of John the Baptist until now the kingdom of heaven suffereth violence, and the violent take it by force."* Matthew 11:12 KJV.

The Jesus that, from the moment he began to preach, preached and ministered the kingdom of God in all its essence and power. What is he saying? That from the moment the prophet spoke of God's kingdom something was released in the atmosphere that made people hungry and responsive to the word of God. In fact, Jesus said that it would cause a forcefulness that would make people crowd in to want to grasp what was offered.

You see, the kingdom of God is on offer in all its realms and dimensions and the Lord releases entrance to the kingdom through declaration and revelation. John started it and Jesus taught the disciples to pray for it:

> *"...your kingdom come, your will be done, on earth as it is in heaven..."* Matthew 6:10

All this, the New Testament and the manifestations of the Spirit have continually directed us to this same kingdom of God. There is nothing passive about Gods kingdom!

This principle is the same for any truth. Abraham was told to see it and then walk it.

> *"The Lord said to Abram after Lot had parted from him, 'Look around from where you are, to the north and south, to the east and west. All the land that you see I will give to you and your offspring forever...Go, walk through the length and breadth of the land, for I am giving it to you.'."*
> Genesis 13:14-15, 17

Equally, any promise offered and any destiny promised must be obtained the same way! Unlike natural inheritance, spiritual inheritance and purpose must be grasped and followed and desired. We must want it, my friends, and want it for real. The spice girls used to sing, "I'll tell you what I want, what I really, really want." That, my friends, was as natural as you could get but the words of that phrase apply and stay with us.

From early in my Christianity I found there was a way into God's purposes. In his grace he has given me visitation after visitation and they all came the same way. DESIRE AND DESIRE, DESIRE THAT BECAME PASSION AND PASSION THAT WOULDN'T TAKE NO FOR AN ANSWER. My wife said to me this morning, "You are not the kind of person that gives in." She used to believe it was because I am Irish by birth and much of my blood. It is not by nationality or culture but rather by the workings of the Spirit of God. I actually preached a message in Georgetown, Texas, last week titled *Never let go of your dream, goal and purpose*. God gives the dream and we pursue it.

Let's speak practicality for a moment. God, wanting to change a man to become a possessor, changes his name!

> *"No longer will you be called Abram; your name will be Abraham!"* Genesis 17:5

There is the destiny proclaimed. Now speak it, say it, proclaim it and pursue it! He did, against all odds! The result? History records both he and Sarah received a miracle in their bodies because he crowded in on his promise. It is time to crowd in on our promise of destiny until the door opens to fulfill it like the father of our faith did. Then we can inherit the same blessings as he did.

> *"So those who rely on faith are blessed along with Abraham, the man of faith."* Galatians 3:9

But you might cry, "This is not my nature!" Maybe not, but it is God's nature! Ask the Holy Spirit to stir up a spirit of Godly violence in you until you possess what is promised!

# CHAPTER 8

# What is That You See

The Lord told Abraham something deeply significant.

> *"Lift up your eyes from where you are and look north and south, east and west. All the land that you see I will give to you and your offspring forever."*
> Genesis 13:14-15 NIV 1984

Until this time Abraham had been a servant and friend but now the Lord wanted to change him into a visionary. One who sees so that he could possess!

The instruction is clear:

*Lift up your eyes!* Look up and look around! Don't be circumstantially based.

*From where you are!* Don't let your present or your past stop you seeing what the Lord wants to show you.

*Look in every direction!* Not just the one. You are not a horse with blinders on or a Christian with just one view but open to every view and every arena.

*Everything you see is yours!* Seeing is possessing! Whatever our vision becomes filled with, we will run after.

What we see, possess and run with affects our offspring, both spiritual and natural. Habakkuk was told,

> *"Write the revelation and make it plain on tablets so that a herald may run with it."* Habakkuk 2:2

Little did Abraham know that the command he was given would open the Godhead, faith and encounter to him. He would see the Christ. He would see his inheritance and he would open the door for us to follow. We must learn that God's method is revelation upon revelation so that we can pursue and gain what we see.

To see, we must look! We must get our heads out of the dirt around us. Like I have always said, we are called to be eagles and not turkeys! We must also not be only open to what we know but rather be open to what we are shown. There was a beautiful old lady in the Pentecostal church I got saved in.. I remember always hearing her pray that God would bless our corner of the vineyard. One day I said to myself, "That is so nice, but Lord what about the rest of the vineyard?" It changed my life as it moved me to desire my full destiny. We must not allow ourselves to be tunnel visioned but open to all he wants to show us so that we can move on into our full destiny!!

This word from God turned Abraham into a man thirsty to see everything he was to see. He wanted to be a possessor! The same passage tells us from that moment he moved his tents!

> *"So Abram moved his tents and went to live near the great trees of Mamre at Hebron, where he built an altar to the Lord."* Genesis 13:18 NIV 1984

He wasn't going to miss out! He actually moved to a place where the *great trees of Mamre* were, meaning *a lusty place or a place filled with passion and vision.*

Are we prepared to reset our gaze? Are we prepared to move from where we are? Are we ready to grasp our heel of destiny? Come on! Start looking again!

# CHAPTER 9

## We Must Not Let Go

In the words of one of the great leaders of the Second World War, "NEVER, NEVER, NEVER GIVE IN!". This is one of the greatest battles of those clinging to their destiny and purpose. Have you noticed that when Jacob was wrestling with the angel he was asked to let go?

> *"Then the man said, 'Let me go, for it is day break.'"* Genesis 32:26

We also find this in 2 Kings 2, where Elisha inherits his mantle from Elijah. Again and again he tries to get Elijah to stay behind. Many a great preacher has preached regarding the places where this happened. What we are wanting to do is show you the pattern. How easily dissuaded are you?

Jacob had to deal with pain. Elisha had to deal with pressure from his spiritual father, Elijah. Look at both of these patriarchs as they leave us such an example to follow. Jacob cries out,

> *"I will not let you go unless you bless me!"*
> Genesis 32:26

Elisha replies in every test,

> *"As surely as the Lord lives and as you live, I will not leave you!"* 2 Kings 2:4

You are not going to put me off!

Abraham is seen doing the same thing in Genesis 18 while wrestling for the life of his nephew, Lot.

What creates such a grasp of the heel of destiny? Firstly, we must know the one who gave the promise, as Abraham did. We must know who he is and that he can do it even in you, whatever your circumstances!

> *"Yet he did not waver through unbelief regarding the promise of God, but was strengthened in his faith and gave glory to God, being fully persuaded that God had power to do what he had promised."*
> Romans 4:20-21

> *"...for he that cometh to God must believe that he is, and that he is a rewarder of them that diligently seek him."* Hebrews 11:6 KJV

This is faith in action!

Secondly, we must allow the Holy Spirit to create in us a tenacity that actually comes from him. The word declares that,

> *"He who began a good work in you will carry it on to completion until the day of Christ Jesus."*
> Philippians 1:6 NIV 1984

He who never gives in creates in us the same spirit and attitude. We see it in sport and in business very often but the ones who should demonstrate this quality should be those touched by his destiny! Thomas Edison who was a famous American inventor, is said to have tried at least 1100 times before he succeeded with the light bulb. Now that is destiny speaking out loud!

Jacob's life work was to gain the blessing he knew was his. Elisha knew that his life would never be fulfilled without gaining what was in his heart. Paul said he was like an athlete reaching for it! He referenced that attitude at least twice, basically declaring that he was running and fighting for a purpose:

> *"I press toward the mark for the prize of the high calling of God in Christ Jesus."* Philippians 3:14

> *"Do you not know that in a race all the runners run, but only one gets the prize? Run in such a way as to get the prize. Everyone who competes in the games goes into strict training. They do it to get a crown that will not last, but we do it to get a crown that will last forever. Therefore I do not run like someone running aimlessly; I do not fight like a boxer beathing the air. No, I strike a blow to my body and make it my slave so that after I have preached to others, I myself will not be disqualified for the prize."* 1 Corinthians 9:24-27

All of them with that one great quality: NEVER, NEVER, NEVER GIVE IN! A man or woman of purpose is just not easily dissuaded. They have the attitude, "That's mine and I know it's mine. I gotta have it. If I fall down, I will get up! If I get beaten in one battle, then I will battle again. If people stand against me, I will sidestep them." We must become armed with this attitude. Then we will gain what has been ours since before we were born. I remember when I was in the British Army in training with the Special Air Service. The greatest thing learned was endurance. The Navy Seals and Marines are the same. In order to become God's special forces we must learn this great truth of endurance, too. Never giving in! No, never giving in. Never letting go! No, never letting go.

# CHAPTER 10

# That Moment of Faith

There is always a moment, when we put to test in faith that which we have received from the Lord! The Bible is full of moments where destiny was grasped. Noah, Jonathan, the early church and Paul. The list goes on.

There was that moment when the mantle dropped down on Elisha in 2 Kings 2:13. That moment when he walked to the water's edge and lifted that mantle up to strike the waters. That moment of launching out, unsure but knowing this was what he had been waiting for! Listen to his cry!

> *"Where now is the Lord, the God of Elijah?"*
> 2 Kings 2:14

There was that moment when, after an encounter once again with the Lord, Abraham uses his new name. That moment when he walks into the camp and tells his wife. Without using his new name he will not prophesy into the air and into his body the word of the Lord!

There was that moment when Ezekiel prophesies to the dry bones:

> *"So I prophesied as I was commanded. And as I was prophesying, there was a noise, a rattling sound, and the bones came together, bone to bone."*
> Ezekiel 37:7

We grab the heel but do we let it grab us? I once asked a famous man who moved in miracles, "When do you feel the anointing? Before you start or after you step out in faith?" His answer? "Very rarely before I start but real soon after I step out in faith." There it is! That moment of putting into practice that which we grabbed hold of.

Let's break down what Elisha actually did when the mantle came down out of the heavens. It is found in that passage in 2 Kings Verses 12-14:

> He first honored the one whom he had served. "My father my father." Honor is always the way to more in God!
>
> In faith he tore off his old mantle or cloak. Why? He was anticipating the new and not expecting to go back. This was a major step in faith indeed!
>
> He picked up the mantle of Elijah from the ground. This was the second great act of faith. He must have thought, "I don't know if it fits, I don't know how to use it but I am picking it up anyway!" There is the faith. I guarantee it was with fear and trembling but his faith said, "Do it! This is the moment I have waited for. I am going for it."
>
> He went back to the Jordan with the mantle and smote the Jordan with it crying out, "Where now is the God of Elijah?". He copied Elijah and called on the God who Elijah served because this was not yet

his experience! I remember that when I was brought into my first deliverance session, I had read what to do but had never done it. What did I do? I copied something I had read that Oral Roberts did but I STILL DID IT! From there I developed my own experience.

He did all of this without a mantle or cloak on, naked as it were. Why? Because that moment of stepping out is naked trust and faith in that which we believed we were going to be given.

I once preached a message called *Grasping God's Moments*. This is so important when that which we dreamed of, prayed for and wrestled to get hold of comes our way. Jacob grasped the heel in the womb, kept grasping until that moment came and then he grasped again and then it became his! Let us be so aware that when our moment comes it will cause us to be thrown into a realm of reaching out in faith.

# CHAPTER 11

# Walking in Destiny's Fulfillment

In Genesis 32, as Jacob limps away from his incredible encounter of blessing from the Lord he realizes that destiny fulfilled can cost us something. The next part of his life was not focused on how much it cost but on walking out the new man. He went into the encounter as Jacob but came out as Israel. Would it have been more comfortable to continue walking as before? This was a new realm. This was a new day. He was carrying a new weight in God. Only in Genesis 35, do we realize how difficult it had been to fully walk into his destiny! From verse 1 thru verse 10, he was still called Jacob but in verse 10, the Lord says, NO MORE! You will be called Israel. This was some time after the encounter and destiny were grasped but now he had to walk it!

Abraham's destiny was in more than just a name. Indeed, that was a prophetic declaration but more so when that child of promise was birthed. Now he had to walk and raise a child who would be the first of the generations that would come through his faith. Abraham, the "father of a multitude", was now beginning to walk his fatherhood out. And what a job he did with his firstborn of promise who feared God and encountered God just as he did. It was one thing to have the desire, then the promise and the gaining of that promise but now here comes the walk. And walk he did. The Lord himself testified,

> *"For I have chosen him, so that he will direct his children and his household after him..."*
> Genesis 18:19

This especially pertains to Elisha's faith moment as he began to walk his destiny. Elijah had passed on. The place of comfort was gone. Now the walk would start. How did he walk out his new prophetic mantle, his destiny grasped? It is all in the ensuing walk.

We must walk this new realm with all its demands. It is not always easy because we always step out beyond where we are! Joshua, the servant of Moses, struggled when the fullness of his destiny came upon him. The Lord had to speak to him sternly in Joshua Chapter one, reminding him that Moses was dead and to not be intimidated to walk out his destiny. Why intimidated? Large shoes to step into, as were Elijah's, Abraham's and many others but now is our moment to be us and not them!

Jesus told Peter,

> *"Launch out into the deep."* Luke 5:4 KJV

There is it is! To step into our destinies and walk them will definitely launch us into the deep way beyond our comfort zone and way into reliance on God himself. Always remember, he has been there before and we have a whole Bible of instances of those who walked before us. History itself exists ready to enlighten us with the lives of others who are examples to us.

Grasping the heel of destiny is more than just a nice dream but, limping as we go, it is a clear walk into the new realms we dreamt of.

# TESTIMONIES

"I met Dennis at Peterborough Bible Week many years ago. During the years that I have known Dennis, not only is he a great friend and man of God, but the prophetic apostolic calling on his life is unique. This incisive, accurate, biblical, prophetic gift not only changes people's lives, but brings tremendous biblical guidance to the government of any local church. Both my wife and I highly recommend Dennis' ministry to any emerging apostolic leadership, local church pastors, and to all those that have a heart of the kingdom. He has been invaluable to the life of our church and our people."   -Steve Maile

"This message comes from a very grateful heart ... a couple years ago, my husband Theo and I were attending Oasis and Pastor Dennis prayed for us to have a baby and prophesied that he could see it growing in my womb. I had a struggle with my faith as we had been trying to conceive for several years without success and I was starting to give up hope. But knowing that God isn't a liar, we held fast to that word, and this month we welcomed our little baby girl, Karina Luna. Thank you for praying for us and releasing faith into our lives and serving as a voice for God's promise. God bless you!"   -Kat S.

"Awesome time (Friday Night, Saturday morning) with Dennis Goldsworthy-Davis. Have not experienced manifestations of the Holy Spirit like that before!! Looking forward to more renewal, revival, restoration Hosea 6:1-3. Bring it on!" -Nigel Reid

# BIOGRAPHY

Dennis Paul Goldsworthy-Davis has been blessed to travel extensively throughout the world ministering both apostolically and prophetically to the body of Christ. He operates within a strong governmental prophetic office and frequently sees the Presence of God and the Spirit of Revival break out upon the lives of people. Dennis has equally been graced to relate to many spiritual sons throughout the earth, bringing wisdom, guidance and encouragement.

Born in Southern Ireland and raised in England, Dennis was radically saved from a life of drugs and violence in 1973. Soon after his conversion, he began to operate within his local church where he was fathered spiritually by Bennie Finch, a seasoned apostolic minister. After working in youth ministry Dennis pastored in several areas within the U.K. It was during these pastorates that Dennis began to see profound moves of God in these same venues.

In 1986 Dennis experienced a dramatic shift in his life and ministry. He and his family moved to San Antonio, Texas, to join a vibrant, functioning apostolic team. In 1990 Dennis was commissioned to start Great Grace International Christian Center, a local work in San Antonio. Dennis continues to serve as the Senior Minister of GGICC and heads the formation of the apostolic team in the local house. Presently, Dennis relates to several functioning apostolic ministries. He draws wisdom and accountability from Robert Henderson of Global Reformers, Barry Wissler of HarvestNet International and for many years, Alan Vincent. Each of these carry strong, well-seasoned apostolic offices in their own right.

Dennis has been married to his wife, Christine, since 1973 and has two wonderful daughters and four grandchildren.

Printed in Great Britain
by Amazon